THE
100+
SERIES™

Reproducible Activities

W9-AGB-462

Brain Games
Mind-Stretching Classroom Activities

Grades 2-3

By
Pat Howard

Cover Design by
Peggy Jackson

Published by Instructional Fair • TS Denison
an imprint of

McGraw-Hill
Children's Publishing

About the Author

Pat Howard has over 30 years of teaching experience. She has taught at many grade levels, ranging from kindergarten through senior high school. Pat is dedicated to the wholistic approach of teaching through individualized instruction, and she has served as a tutor to many homebound children. Ms. Howard has spent much of the last eight years designing materials for homebound presentation and has a number of published activity books. She lives in Delta, British Columbia, Canada with her family and Irish setter, Spencer.

Credits

Author: Pat Howard
Cover Design: Peggy Jackson
Project Director/Editor: Jerry Aten
Editors: Stephanie Garcia, Mary Hassinger
Page Design: Peggy Jackson
Page Production: Lentz Design, C.J. Designs

McGraw-Hill
Children's Publishing

A Division of The **McGraw·Hill** *Companies*

Published by Instructional Fair • TS Denison
An imprint of McGraw-Hill Children's Publishing
Copyright © 2002 McGraw-Hill Children's Publishing

Send all inquiries to:
McGraw-Hill Children's Publishing
3195 Wilson Drive NW
Grand Rapids, Michigan 49544

Brain Games—grades 2-3
ISBN: 0-7424-0211-8

1 2 3 4 5 6 7 8 9 07 06 05 04 03 02

Table of Contents

To the Teacher

Introduction

The music teacher says he will be ten minutes late in arriving to your classroom today; a small group of students finishes a project early; or your best reader completes her literature assignment ahead of class again. Don't panic! There is no reason for learners to be bored or disruptive when they discover a few "free" minutes. ***BRAIN GAMES*** can engage your students in challenging and fun brain exercises while they wait to start the next lesson.

BRAIN GAMES is divided into three main sections: ***Individual Amusement***, ***Partner Play***, and ***Entire-Class Games***. Games in the ***Individual Amusement*** and ***Partner Play*** sections are designed to allow students who finish their work early to play educational games without the assistance of a teacher. ***Entire-Class Games*** are designed to engage your entire class in meaningful activities led either by a teacher or a student.

Preparing for play with ***BRAIN GAMES*** is easy:

1. Set up a file folder for each game. Reproduce the game's instruction sheet and attach it to the file folder.

2. If there are game boards or playing pieces included for the game, reproduce enough copies for several students to play and store them in the file folder.

3. Place the file folders in a storage box and organize them into sections for individuals, partners, or whole class activities.

4. Place additional playing materials such as dice, decks of playing cards, and counters in the box.

5. Store the box in an area of the classroom that is accessible to your students and define the rules for when and how they can use the materials.

Now you and your students are ready to fill in those extra minutes whenever they become available.

Brain Games
Individual Amusement

Instructions

Spell-A-Thon

Players: One

Materials: Spell-A-Thon worksheet, pencil, sand timer

Goal: Write as many words as possible from a set of letters.

Rules:
1. Choose ten consonants and two vowels. Write them at the top of your worksheet.
2. Turn over the sand timer.
3. Using the letters you chose, write as many words on your worksheet as you can. Each letter may be used more than once, but only once within each word.
4. Stop writing when the timer stops.
5. Use a dictionary to check the spelling of any words that you are not sure of.
6. Give yourself a score for every word you spelled correctly. Consonants are worth two points and vowels are worth one point.
7. Add your total points to get your final score.

Language Arts

Spell-A-Thon

Write ten consonants.

Write two vowels.

Words	Points per word	Words	Points per word
_____	_____	_____	_____
_____	_____	_____	_____
_____	_____	_____	_____
_____	_____	_____	_____
_____	_____	_____	_____
_____	_____	_____	_____
_____	_____	_____	_____
_____	_____	_____	_____
_____	_____	_____	_____

Total points for column 1_____

Total points for column 2_____

Final score (grand total)_____

Players: One

Materials: Positive Connections game board, pencil

Goal: To create number paths from the top of the game board to the bottom.

Rules:
1. Fill in the grid with numbers 1 to 40. Place the numbers in any order you want.
2. Decide if you will make your paths using odd numbers or even numbers.
3. Choose a number from the top row of the grid. Draw a line from that number to another number that is connected to it. Lines can go across, down, or diagonally.
4. Continue connecting numbers until you get to the bottom of the grid. All of the numbers in the path should be either odd or even.
5. Go back to the top of the grid and make another path. Any number that was used in the first path cannot be used again. New lines cannot cross over old lines.

29	5	22	2	15	26	11	30
13	37	1	32	20	33	36	19
24	6	28	4	3	16	7	31
37	17	27	9	14	35	23	38
25	18	10	21	8	34	12	40

21	8	1	15	22	3	26	11
30	13	28	2	6	34	10	35
12	31	9	25	24	16	20	39
29	18	23	14	4	19	27	38
37	5	32	33	17	7	36	40

Critical Thinking

Positive Connections

Players: One

Materials:
Materials: eight one-inch squares of red paper, eight one-inch squares of blue paper, red crayon, blue crayon, Swap Spots game board

Goal:
Reverse the positions of the playing pieces on the game board.

Rules:
1. Color the squares on the game board like this:

red	red	red		
red	red	red		
red	red		blue	blue
		blue	blue	blue
		blue	blue	blue

2. Place the blue squares of paper on the red spaces. Place the red squares of paper on the blue spaces.
3. Move one square at a time into a new space. You may move across, up and down, and diagonally. The game pieces cannot jump over any spaces.
4. The game is over when you have moved all of the blue squares to the blue spaces and all of the red squares to the red spaces.

Critical Thinking

Swap Spots

11

Add It Up

Players: One

Materials: Add It Up game board

Goal: To place three cards in a row that add up to 21.

Rules:
1. Cut apart the number cards on the game board.
2. Shuffle the cards and place them facedown in a pile.
3. Draw the first card from the pile and place it anywhere on the game board.
4. Draw another card and place it on the game board. As you add cards to the game board, total the sums of the cards that are in rows or columns.
5. Keep playing until you have a row or a column that adds up to 21.
6. Choose a new number and play again.

Math

Add It Up

✂- -

1	2	3	4	5	6
7	8	9	1	2	3
4	5	6	7	8	9

Instructions

Odd and Even

Players: One

Materials: Two dice, Odd and Even worksheet, pencil

Goal: Estimate the number of times an odd number will be rolled and the number of times an even number will be rolled and test your predictions.

Rules:
1. You are going to roll the dice 15 times. Guess how many times the sum of the numbers rolled will be odd and how many times the sum will be even. Write your predictions on the worksheet.
2. Roll the dice. Write the number of each die on the worksheet. Add the two numbers together and write the sum. Circle **Odd** or **Even**.
3. Continue rolling the dice until you have rolled 15 times.
4. Write the actual totals of odd rolls and even rolls at the bottom of the worksheet.
5. Rank how accurate your predictions were.

Odd and Even

Out of 15 rolls, how many times do you think you will roll an odd number?
Out of 15 rolls, how many times do you think you will roll an even number?

	Die 1	Die 2	Sum	Odd or Even?
1.				Odd Even
2.				Odd Even
3.				Odd Even
4.				Odd Even
5.				Odd Even
6.				Odd Even
7.				Odd Even
8.				Odd Even
9.				Odd Even
10.				Odd Even
11.				Odd Even
12.				Odd Even
13.				Odd Even
14.				Odd Even
15.				Odd Even

Total number of odd sums: _____

Total number of even sums:_____

My predictions were:

Right On   Pretty Close   Far Off

Dollar Days

Players: One

Materials: Dollar Days worksheet, pencil

Goal: Each letter of the alphabet is given a dollar amount. Use the dollar amount to estimate the "price" of different words. Then add the amounts up to find the actual price.

Rules:
1. Read the chart below to see how much each letter is worth.
2. Look at the Dollar Days worksheet. Write the words and the dollar amounts for each letter. Add up the total dollar amount for each word.

A	B	C	D	E	F	G
$1.00	$2.00	$3.00	$4.00	$5.00	$6.00	$7.00
H	I	J	K	L	M	N
$8.00	$9.00	$10.00	$11.00	$12.00	$13.00	$14.00
O	P	Q	R	S	T	U
$15.00	$16.00	$17.00	$18.00	$19.00	$20.00	$21.00
V	W	X	Y	Z		
$22.00	$23.00	$24.00	$25.00	$26.00		

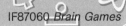

Math

Dollar Days

Use the chart on the Dollar Days Instructions sheet to complete the exercises below.

Total Price

1. Find the price of your name.

_____   _____

2. Find the price of a classmate's name.

_____   _____

3. Find the price of your teacher's name.

_____   _____

4. Find the price of your school's name.

_____   _____

5. Find the price of the title of your favorite book.

_____   _____

6. Write a word with a price of $10.

_____   _____

7. Write a word with a price of $50.

_____   _____

8. Write a word with a price of $100.

_____   _____

Fast Facts

Players: One

Materials: One deck of cards with the face cards removed, sand timer

Goal: Practice addition or multiplication facts.

Rules:

1. Shuffle the deck of cards. Place them in a pile facedown.
2. Turn the sand timer over to start the clock.
3. Flip the first two cards in the pile over. Add or multiply the numbers together.
4. Repeat step three until the timer stops. Count how many problems you were able to solve.
5. Set the timer again and play another round with the remaining cards. See if you can solve more problems with each round that you play.

Brain Games

Partner Play

IF87060 *Brain Games*

Draw It

Players: Four

Materials: Draw It worksheet, sand timer, pencil, paper

Goal: Guess the picture drawn by your partner.

Rules:

1. The game is played with two teams. Two players are on each team.
2. Cut the score sheet portion from the Draw It worksheet. Set it aside.
3. Cut apart the game cards. Shuffle the cards and place them facedown in a pile.
4. A player from Team 1 takes the first card from the pile and silently reads the word. A player from Team 2 turns the sand timer over.
5. The player on Team 1 who chose the card draws pictures so that his or her partner can guess the word on the game card. No words, letters, or numbers may be used in the drawing. The player drawing the pictures may not speak. The second player on the team must guess what the word is before the sand in the timer runs out.
6. If the word is guessed correctly, Team 1 scores a point.
7. When time is up, one player on Team 2 gets to choose a game card and draw pictures for his or her partner.
8. Players take turns choosing game cards and drawing pictures. The team with the most points at the end of the playing time wins.

Language Arts

Draw It

study	read	write
add	subtract	run
jump	draw	talk
think	book	game
science	math	skip
hop	throw	catch
art	music	

Score Card	
Team 1	Team 2

Instructions

Build-a-Word

Players: Two

Materials: Build-a-Word worksheet, two different colored pencils

Goal: Spell as many words as possible on the worksheet.

Rules:
1. The first player writes a letter in a box on the worksheet.
2. The second player adds a letter to the worksheet. The new letter must be written in a box that touches the first box.
3. Players take turns adding one letter at a time to the worksheet. Each new letter must be in a box that touches another box with a letter.
4. When a player adds a letter that completes a word, he or she circles the word with his or her colored pencil. Words can go across, down, or diagonally.
5. The game is over when no new letters can be added. The player who circled the most words wins the game.

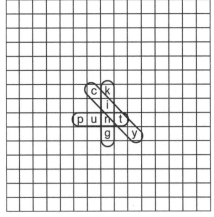

IF87060 *Brain Games*

Language Arts

Build-a-Word

THE	MY	MAKE	WITH	HIS	MORE	FIND

GET	THEM	FROM	LOOK	HER	TIME

IF87060 *Brain Games*

Letter Lotto

Players: Four

Materials: One Letter Lotto game board for each player, pencils

Goal: Use spelling skills to create words on the game board.

Rules:

1. The first player calls out any letter of the alphabet. All players write the letter in any space on their game boards.
2. The second player calls out any letter. Again, all players write the letter in any space on the game boards.
3. Each player is to try to use the letters to create words on his or her game board. When a word is created, the player circles the word. Words can go across, down, or diagonally.
4. When all of the squares on the game boards are filled, players can search for any additional words they created but did not circle. Players should circle all words that they find.
5. Each player lists the circled words on the back of his or her game board. Each word gets a point equal to the number of letters used in the word. For example, a three-letter word gets three points.
6. Players exchange game boards to check the spelling and points for each word. The player with the most points wins.

Name _____
Date _____

Name _____
Date _____

Name _____
Date _____

Name _____
Date _____

25 IF87060 *Brain Games*

Instructions

Fishing for Letters

Players: Two to Four

Materials: Four sets of the Fishing for Letters cards

Goal: Create as many words as possible using the letter cards.

Rules:

1. Cut apart the letter cards. You should have four cards for each letter of the alphabet.
2. Shuffle the cards. Deal five cards facedown to each player. Place the rest of the cards facedown in a pile.
3. Each player looks at his or her cards. If any words can be created from the cards, the player places the cards faceup so the other players can see them. Words must be at least three letters long.
4. Each letter has a point value. As words are created, players add up the point values to get their scores.
5. The first player chooses one other player and asks for a letter. If that player has the letter, he or she must give it to the person who asked for it and then draw a new card. If the player does not have the letter, he or she tells the person, "Fish for a letter." The first player then draws a card from the pile.
6. Players take turns asking for new letters. Each time a player can create a word with at least three letters, he or she places the cards faceup so the other players can see the word.
7. The game is over when there are no more cards in the pile. The players add up their points. The player with the most points wins.

Language Arts

Fishing for Letters

a 1	b 2	c 2	d 2	e 1
f 2	g 2	h 3	i 1	j 3
k 3	l 2	m 2	n 2	o 1
p 2	q 3	r 2	s 2	t 2
u 1	v 3	w 3	x 3	y 3
z 3				

IF87060 *Brain Games*

Sharing Thoughts

Players: Two

Materials: Paper, pencil

Goal: Practice speaking and listening skills.

Rules:

1. Players sit with their backs facing each other.
2. The first player chooses an object in the room and writes the name of that object on a sheet of paper.
3. The first player gives one clue about the object and the second player tries to guess what it is.
4. Only five clues may be given. If the second player names the object after the first clue, he or she scores one point. If the object is named after the second clue, two points are scored. Scoring continues up to five points. If the object is not named after five clues, the first player tells what the object is and the second player scores five points.
5. Players take turns at guessing the objects. The player with the lowest score at the end of the playing time wins.

Instructions

Story Time

Players: Two to Four

Materials: Ruler

Goal: Share in telling a group story.

Rules:
1. The player holding the ruler is the storyteller.
2. The storyteller chooses a folktale or fairy tale to start the story. The storyteller can make as many changes to the original story as he or she wants. After a few sentences, the ruler is passed to the next player.
3. The second player then becomes the storyteller. He or she picks up the story where the last player left off. The new storyteller adds a few sentences to the story, then passes the ruler to the next player.
4. Play continues until the story reaches its conclusion.
5. A new story can be started if time allows.

Five-in-a-Row

Players: Two

Materials: Two different colored pencils, sheet of graph paper

Goal: Use thinking skills to plan strategies for blocking opponent's path

Rules:
1. One player will use an X for his or her mark. The other player will use an O.
2. The first player draws his or her mark in a square. Then the second player takes a turn.
3. When a player has five marks in a row, he or she circles the marks and scores five points. Rows of marks can go across, up and down, and diagonally.
4. Players should try to block each other from drawing five marks in a row.
5. The player with the most points at the end of the playing time wins.

Map Makers

Players: 2 per team

Materials: Paper and pencil for each team, five objects for each team

Goal: Make and read maps.

Rules:
1. Each team will select five objects and hide them around the school grounds.
2. The team will then draw a map to show where each object is hidden.
3. Teams exchange maps and try to find each other's objects.
4. For every object that is found using the maps, the team that hid it scores a point. If an object is found without the use of the map, the team that hid it does not score a point.
5. The team with the most points at the end of the playing time wins.

Path to Victory

Players: Two

Materials: Path to Victory game board, two different colored pencils

Goal: Use thinking skills to draw paths from the top of the game board to the bottom.

Rules:

1. One player will use the Xs on the game board. The other player will use the Os.
2. The first player must connect two of his or her letters by drawing a line between them.
3. The second player then draws a line between two of his or her letters.
4. Players take turns drawing lines. Lines can be drawn between any two matching letters that are next to each other. They can go across or up and down. Diagonal lines are not allowed.
5. Lines can not be drawn through other lines.
6. The first player to make a connected line from the top row of his or her letters to the bottom row wins the game.

Critical Thinking

Path to Victory

X		X		X		X		X	
	O		O		O		O		O
X		X		X		X		X	
	O		O		O		O		O
X		X		X		X		X	
	O		O		O		O		O
X		X		X		X		X	
	O		O		O		O		O
X		X		X		X		X	
	O		O		O		O		O

Instructions

Absolute Lines

Players: Two

Materials: Absolute Lines game board, two different colored pencils

Goal: Use thinking skills to plan moves for the game.

Rules:
1. The first player will draw a left-right line through two squares on the game board.
2. The second player will draw an up-down line through two squares.
3. Players will draw their lines in the same way for each turn.
4. A line can not be drawn in any square that already has a line.
5. Play continues until one player cannot draw any more lines. The other player is the winner.

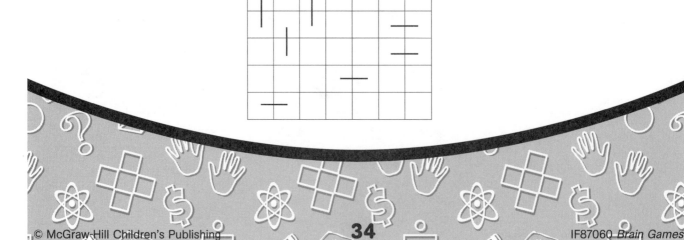

IF87060 *Brain Games*

Critical Thinking

Absolute Lines

Take the Test

Players: Two

Materials: Take the Test game board, 16 game counters (beans, stones, or other small objects will work)

Goal: Use thinking skills to plan moves for the game.

Rules:
1. Place a counter in each square on the game board.
2. Players take turns removing one counter from the game board at a time.
3. To remove a counter, its square must have one side touching another square that still holds a counter.
4. The game can only be won if there is only one counter left on the game board. If there is more than one counter left that cannot be removed, the game is over and players start again.

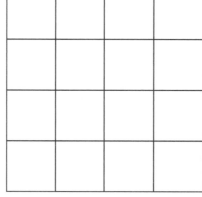

Name _____

Date _____

<table>
<tr><td></td><td></td><td></td><td></td></tr>
<tr><td></td><td></td><td></td><td></td></tr>
<tr><td></td><td></td><td></td><td></td></tr>
<tr><td></td><td></td><td></td><td></td></tr>
</table>

- ✂

Name _____

Date _____

<table>
<tr><td></td><td></td><td></td><td></td></tr>
<tr><td></td><td></td><td></td><td></td></tr>
<tr><td></td><td></td><td></td><td></td></tr>
<tr><td></td><td></td><td></td><td></td></tr>
</table>

IF87060 *Brain Games*

Instructions
Snake in the Grass

Players: Two

Materials: Snake in the Grass game board, two different colored pencils

Goal: Use thinking skills to link the dots.

Rules:
1. The first player circles a dot on the game board. The circled dot becomes the snake's head. The player then draws a line from the head to another dot to begin the snake's tail.
2. Players take turns linking dots one at a time. Lines between the dots can go across or up and down. Diagonal lines are not allowed.
3. The player who is forced to connect the tail of the snake back to itself, loses the game.

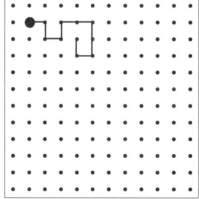

Critical Thinking

Snake in the Grass

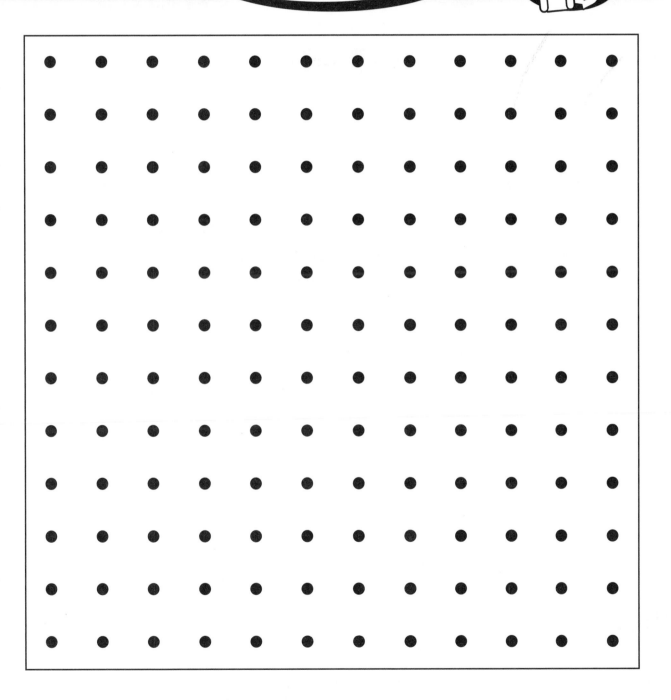

Instructions

Jumping Beans

Players: Two

Materials: Jumping Beans game board, beans

Goal: Use thinking skills to collect as many beans as possible from the game board.

Rules:
1. Place a bean in each square on the game board. Do not place a bean in the middle square.
2. The first player moves one bean over another bean to land in the empty square. The player removes the bean that was jumped over from the game board.
3. The second player takes a turn and removes the bean that was jumped.
4. Players continue taking turns until no more jumps are possible.
5. The player who collects the most beans wins.

IF87060 *Brain Games*

Critical Thinking

Jumping Beans

Making Connections

Players: Two

Materials: Making Connections game board, two different colored pencils

Goal: Connect the dots to complete geometric shapes.

Rules:
1. Players take turns connecting two dots at a time on the game board.
2. Lines can be drawn across, up and down, and diagonally.
3. Players can add on to each other's lines.
4. The player who adds the last line to create a shape writes his or her initials in the shape.
5. The player with the most shapes at the end of the playing time wins.

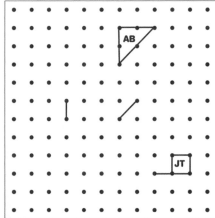

Critical Thinking

Making Connections

Players: Two

Materials: Strategy game board, three playing pieces for each player, two different colored crayons

Goal: Use thinking skills to place all three playing pieces in a row.

Rules:
1. Players cut out the playing pieces. Each player colors his or her playing pieces one color.
2. Players take turns putting one playing piece on the game board at a time.
3. Playing pieces do not have to be placed near each other.
4. Once all six playing pieces are on the game board, players will take turns moving one piece at a time. Pieces may be moved up and down, across, and diagonally one space at a time. No jumping is allowed.
5. The first player to get all of his or her playing pieces lined up in a row wins.

Critical Thinking

Strategy

Two Will Do

Players: Two to Four

Materials: One deck of playing cards

Goal: Match playing cards to the last card played and be the first player to run out of cards.

Rules:

1. Shuffle the cards and deal seven cards to each player. Place the remaining cards facedown in a pile.
2. Turn the first card in the pile over and place it to the side to start the discard pile. The number and suit shown on the card must now be matched. For example, if the five of diamonds is drawn, the first player must place either a five or another diamond card on top of the discard pile.
3. Twos are wild. This means that a two can be played at any time, regardless of the suit or the number showing.
4. If a player does not have a card that matches the suit or number needed, he or she must draw cards from the pile until a match is found.
5. Players take turns matching or drawing cards.
6. The first player to discard all of the cards in his or her hand wins.

Up and Down

Players: Four

Materials: One deck of playing cards

Goal: Play cards that are one number greater than or one number less than the card showing.

Rules:

1. Shuffle the cards and divide them evenly between the players.
2. A player who has a number 7 begins the game by placing the 7 faceup in the middle of the playing area.
3. The next player must choose a number from the same suit that is either one greater than 7 or one less than 7. If the player does not have a card that can be played, he or she can play a 7 from another suit. This will change the suit that must be played.
4. Players take turns adding cards that are one greater than or one less than the last card played. If a player cannot make a play, he or she misses a turn.
5. The first player to discard all of the cards in his or her hand wins.

Players: Two

Materials: Secret Number game board for each player, pencils

Goal: Use greater than and less than clues to guess the secret number.

Rules:
1. Players sit with their backs facing each other.
2. Each player thinks of a secret number between 1 and 10 and writes it down on the back of his or her game board.
3. The players take turns giving clues and guessing each other's numbers. Clues must use greater than or less than statements. For example, "My number is greater than 2." Or, "My number is less than 5 + 3."
4. Three clues can be given for each secret number.
5. If a player guesses his or her opponent's secret number with three clues or less, he or she colors in a space in the row with that number on the game board. If the number is not guessed, the player giving the clues fills in that space on his or her game board.
6. The player with the most boxes filled in on his or her game board at the end of the playing time wins.

Secret Number

Name _____   **Date**_____

1										
2										
3										
4										
5										
6										
7										
8										
9										
10										

IF87060 *Brain Games*

Odd and Even

Players: Two

Materials: Odd and Even game board, one pair of dice, two different colored crayons

Goal: Roll the dice and move through the game board.

Rules:
1. Players cut out the playing pieces. Each player colors his or her playing piece one color.
2. Players take turns rolling the dice.
3. If two even numbers are rolled, the player moves one space on the game board.
4. If two odd numbers are rolled, the player moves two spaces.
5. If one odd number and one even number is rolled, the player moves three spaces.
6. If doubles are rolled, the player loses a turn.
7. The first player to reach the end of the game board wins.

Math

Odd and Even

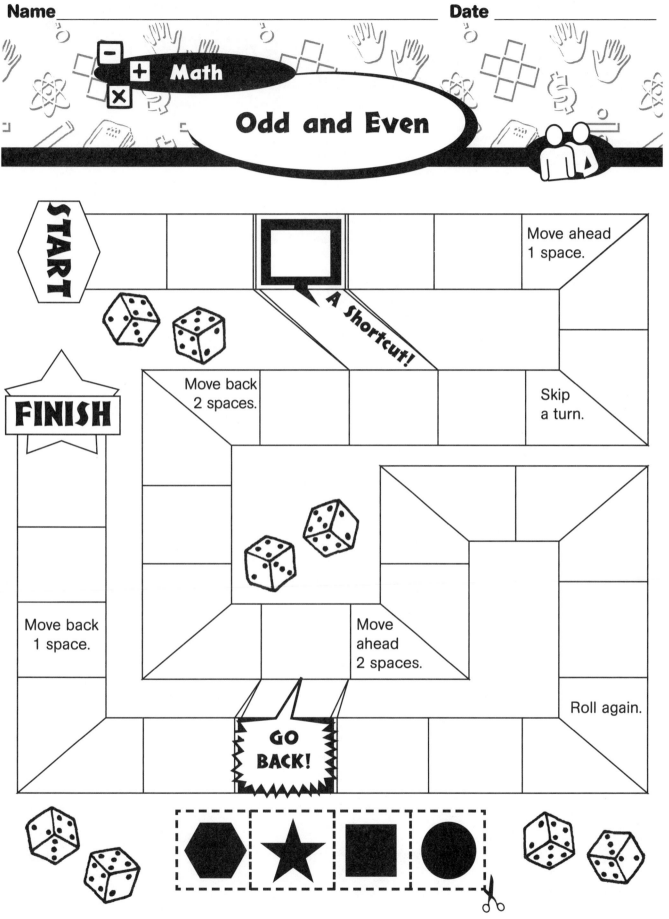

START

FINISH

A Shortcut!

Move ahead 1 space.

Move back 2 spaces.

Skip a turn.

Move back 1 space.

Move ahead 2 spaces.

Roll again.

GO BACK!

51

Instructions

Addition Adventure

Players: Two to Four

Materials: Addition Adventure game board, three dice, three different sets of game markers for each player (beans, paper scraps, small pasta noodles, etc.)

Goal: Roll the dice, add the numbers, and cover a matching number on the game board.

Rules:
1. Players take turns rolling the three dice and finding the sum of the numbers.
2. The player who rolled the dice then looks for the sum on the game board. The player covers the sum with one of his or her markers.
3. Play continues until all of the numbers on the game board are covered. The player who covered the most numbers wins.

 **Math**

Addition Adventure

18

3 **12**

17 **8** **15**

9 **16** **13** **7**

13 **11** **5** **18** **14**

14 **6** **10** **15** **5** **8**

10 **11** **9** **7** **16** **12** **4**

53

Pick a Number

Players: Four

Materials: One deck of playing cards

Goal: Collect cards that will add up to a certain sum.

Rules:
1. One player is chosen as the dealer. He or she chooses a sum for the game between 11 and 50. Then the dealer shuffles the cards and deals five cards facedown to each player.
2. Each player looks at his or her cards and adds up the numbers. Face cards are worth 10 points each. If a player has the sum chosen by the dealer, he or she shows the cards and wins the game. If no one has the sum, the game continues.
3. Each player chooses one card from his or her hand and passes it facedown to the person on the left.
4. The players pick up their new cards and find the sums of their new hands.
5. The first player to get the correct sum wins the game.

Double-Digit Duo

Players: Two

Materials: One deck of playing cards with face cards removed, paper, two pencils, calculator

Goal: Use playing cards to create two-digit numbers and add the numbers together.

Rules:

1. Shuffle the cards and place them facedown in a pile.
2. The first player draws four cards from the pile. He or she uses the cards to make two two-digit numbers and adds the numbers together.
3. The second player takes a turn drawing cards, creating two-digit numbers, and adding the numbers together.
4. Players can check their math using the calculator. The player with the largest sum collects all the cards for that hand.
5. The game continues until there are no more cards in the pile. The player who collected the most cards wins.

Royal Square

Players: Two

Materials: Royal Square game board, Royal Square flash cards, one pair of dice, about 30 game markers for each player (beans, pennies, pasta noodles, etc. Each player needs his or her own kind of marker.)

Goal: Cover as many numbers on the game board as possible.

Rules:
1. Cut apart the flash cards, shuffle them, and place them facedown in a pile.
2. Fill in the game board with numbers 1 to 30. The numbers can be written in any order.
3. The first player rolls the dice and adds the two digits together. Then the player draws a flash card from the pile. If the flash card says "greater than," the player covers a number on the game board that is greater than the sum of the numbers rolled. If the flash card says "less than," he or she covers a number that is less than the sum of the numbers rolled.
4. The second player then takes a turn.
5. If a player cannot cover a new number on the game board, that player misses a turn.
6. Play continues until all of the numbers on the game board are covered. The player who covered the most numbers wins.

Math

Royal Square

57

IF87060 *Brain Games*

GREATER THAN	GREATER THAN	LESS THAN	LESS THAN
GREATER THAN	GREATER THAN	LESS THAN	LESS THAN
GREATER THAN	GREATER THAN	LESS THAN	LESS THAN
GREATER THAN	GREATER THAN	LESS THAN	LESS THAN
GREATER THAN	GREATER THAN	LESS THAN	LESS THAN

Zero Wins

Players: Two

Materials: One pair of dice, a sheet of paper, pencil

Goal: Starting at 100, use addition and subtraction skills to get to zero.

Rules:

1. Fold a sheet of paper in half. Write the name of the first player on the left side of the paper. Write the name of the second player on the right side of the paper. Write 100 under each name.
2. The first player rolls the dice and adds the two numbers together. The player writes the number on his or her side of the paper and subtracts it from 100.
3. The second player then takes a turn.
4. Players continue rolling the dice and subtracting the sum of the numbers from the last number on the score sheet.
5. The first player to get to zero wins.

Sum It Up

Players: Two to Four

Materials: Sum It Up number strips, pencils, one pair of dice, sheet of paper

Goal: Cross out as many numbers on the number strip as possible.

Rules:

1. Cut apart the number strips. Each player takes one strip to start the game.
2. The first player rolls the dice. On the number strip, the player can either cross out the two numbers that were rolled or the sum of the numbers rolled.
3. Players take turns rolling the dice and crossing out numbers on their number strips.
4. If the numbers and their sums have already been crossed out, the player misses a turn. If a player misses three turns in a row, he or she is out of the round.
5. When the last player misses a turn three times in a row, the round is over. The players add up the numbers that are not crossed out on their number strips to get a score.
6. Write the scores on a sheet of paper and start again with new number strips. The player with the lowest score at the end of all of the rounds wins the game.

Math

Sum It Up

1	2	3	4	5	6	7	8	9	10	11	12
1	2	3	4	5	6	7	8	9	10	11	12
1	2	3	4	5	6	7	8	9	10	11	12
1	2	3	4	5	6	7	8	9	10	11	12
1	2	3	4	5	6	7	8	9	10	11	12
1	2	3	4	5	6	7	8	9	10	11	12
1	2	3	4	5	6	7	8	9	10	11	12
1	2	3	4	5	6	7	8	9	10	11	12
1	2	3	4	5	6	7	8	9	10	11	12
1	2	3	4	5	6	7	8	9	10	11	12
1	2	3	4	5	6	7	8	9	10	11	12
1	2	3	4	5	6	7	8	9	10	11	12
1	2	3	4	5	6	7	8	9	10	11	12
1	2	3	4	5	6	7	8	9	10	11	12

IF87060 *Brain Games*

Instructions

Crazy Coordinates

Players: Two

Materials: Crazy Coordinates game board, one pair of red dice, one pair of white dice, two different colored pencils, scrap paper

Goal: Plot the most coordinates on the graph.

Rules:
1. The first player rolls all four dice. He or she adds the two red dice together and writes the sum on scrap paper. That player then adds the two white dice together and writes the sum on the scrap paper.
2. The sums are used as coordinates. The player marks the graph where the two sums meet.
3. The second player follows the same steps.
4. If a coordinate has already been marked, the player may reverse the order of the numbers. If that coordinate has already been marked, the player loses his or her turn.
5. The player with the most coordinates marked at the end of the playing time wins.

Math

Crazy Coordinates

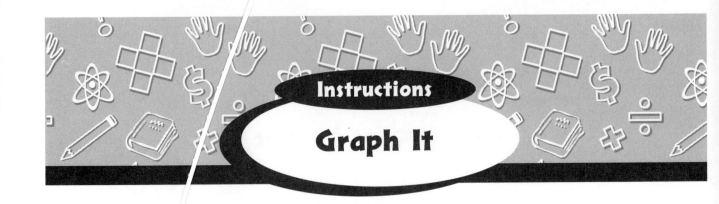

Players: Two to Four

Materials: Graph It game board, one deck of cards with the face cards removed, two different colored pencils

Goal: Write addition sentences on the graph.

Rules:
1. Shuffle the cards and place them facedown in a pile.
2. The first player draws two cards and adds the numbers together. He or she finds the sum on the graph and writes the number sentence in that row.
3. Players take turns drawing cards and writing number sentences on the graph. Once a number sentence has been written on the graph, it cannot be used again.
4. The player with the most number sentences recorded on the graph at the end of the playing time wins.

Math

Graph It

2
3
4
5
6
7
8
9
10
11
12
13
14
15
16
17
18
19
20

Instructions

Finders Keepers

Players: Two

Materials: One deck of playing cards with the face cards removed, one pair of dice

Goal: Use addition to collect the most cards.

Rules:
1. Shuffle cards. Arrange the cards in rows, faceup.
2. The first player rolls the dice and adds the numbers together. Then the player looks for the sum in the rows of playing cards. If the sum is found, the player takes the card.
3. Players continue taking turns rolling the dice and collecting cards.
4. Only one card can be taken during each turn.
5. If a card matching the sum of the dice cannot be found, that player loses a turn.
6. The player with the most cards at the end of the playing time wins.

Multiplication Snap

Players: Two

Materials: One deck of playing cards with the face cards removed

Goal: Multiply the numbers on the cards.

Rules:
1. Shuffle the cards. Deal them evenly between the players.
2. Each player keeps his or her cards facedown in a pile.
3. At the same time, each player flips the top card from his or her pile over.
4. The first player to multiply the two numbers together and call out the correct answer keeps the cards.
5. If there is a tie, the cards go into a discard pile.
6. The player with the most cards at the end of the playing time wins.

Rolling Along

Players: Two

Materials: Rolling Along game board for each player, one pair of dice, two different colored pencils

Goal: Multiply numbers and cross out numbers on the game board.

Rules:

1. The first player rolls the dice and multiplies the two numbers to find the product. Next, the player looks at the game board. He or she can cross out the product or any two numbers that can be multiplied to arrive at the same product.

    Example: If 3 and 4 are rolled, the product is 12 (3 x 4 = 12).
    The player can cross out a 12 on the game board or any of the following pairs of numbers:
    1 and 12 (1 x 12 = 12)
    2 and 6 (2 x 6 = 12)
    3 and 4 (3 x 4 = 12)

2. Players take turns rolling the dice, multiplying the numbers, and crossing out numbers on the game board.
3. If a player cannot cross out any numbers, he or she loses a turn.
4. The player with the most numbers crossed out on the game board at the end of the playing time wins.

Math

Rolling Along

19	12	39	10	2	35
11	22	16	24	38	3
33	13	36	9	30	18
4	26	20	23	27	7
32	6	25	15	34	1
17	21	14	8	5	31

Quick Draw Relay

Players: Four

Materials: One set of math flashcards

Goal: Answer math problems as quickly as possible.

Rules:
1. Players play in teams of two.
2. Shuffle the flashcards and place them facedown in a pile.
3. The first two players for each team face the pile. The second player from one of the teams flips the first card in the pile over.
4. The first player to answer the problem correctly wins the card for his or her team.
5. The second two players then take a turn.
6. Play continues until there are no more cards left in the pile.
7. The team with the most cards wins.

Instructions

Multiplication Madness

Players: Two to four

Materials: Multiplication Madness game board, one pair of dice, game marker for each player (pasta noodle, penny, bean, etc.), calculator

Goal: Solve math problems to get to the end of the game board.

Rules:
1. Glue each page of the game board onto the inside of a file folder.
2. All players place their game markers on "Start".
3. The first player rolls the dice and moves that number of spaces on the game board. Then the player multiplies the number of spaces he or she moved by the number that is shown on the new space. Other players may use the calculator to check the answer. If the answer is correct, the player stays on the new space. If it is incorrect, the player must go back to his or her last space.
4. Players take turns moving along the game board.
5. The first player to reach the end wins the game.

Math

Multiplication Madness

4
2
10
7
1
5
3

0
6
8
11

7
5
3
10
9
12

START

FINISH

7
8
1
6
10
9
12
2
8
5
4
7

IF87060 Brain Games

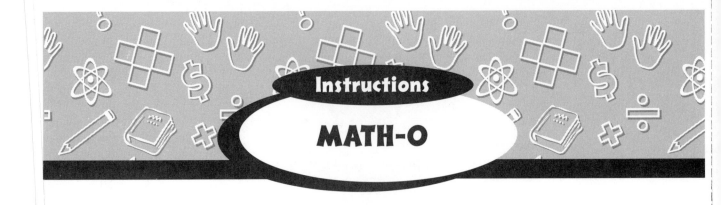

MATH-O

Players: Four

Materials: One MATH-O board for each player, pencils, one pair of red dice, one pair of white dice, about 25 one-inch squares of scrap paper for each player

Goal: Multiply and cover five spaces in a row on the MATH-O board.

Rules:
1. Each player fills in numbers on his or her MATH-O board. Numbers must be between 4 and 144. The player should choose numbers that will be the answers of two numbers multiplied together.
2. The first player calls out a letter from the MATH-O board, then rolls all four dice. He or she finds the sum of the red dice and multiplies it by the sum of the white dice.
3. All players check their MATH-O boards. If the answer to the multiplication problem is in the column under the letter that the player called out, the number is covered with a scrap of paper.

Example: The player called out the letter "M" in MATH-O.
   The red dice show 2 and 6. 2 + 6 = 8.
   The white dice show 3 and 1. 3 + 1 = 4.
   Multiply 8 and 4. 8 x 4 = 32.
   Any player that has a 32 written under the "M" on the MATH-O board covers up the number with a piece of scrap paper.

4. Players take turns calling out a letter, rolling the dice, and solving the multiplication problems.
5. The first player to have five numbers covered in a row calls out "MATH-O" and wins the game.

Math

MATH-O

M	A	T	H	O
		FREE SPACE		

IF87060 *Brain Games*

Players: Two to Four

Materials: Rock and Roll game board, two small cubes, pencil and paper for each player, calculator

Goal: Add or subtract numbers on the game board to earn a score.

Rules:
1. Players decide if they will practice addition or subtraction during the game.
2. The first player rolls the cubes on the game board. Then that player adds or subtracts the numbers that the cubes landed on. The player uses the calculator to check the answer. If the player gave the correct answer, that player writes it on the paper.
3. Players take turns rolling the dice, adding or subtracting the numbers, and writing their scores.
4. At the end of the playing time, the players add all of the numbers on their papers. The player with the highest score wins.

Math

Rock and Roll

10	30	38	18	6
28	3	40	23	17
39	15	37	9	13
19	22	4	27	31
33	26	36	16	2
5	11	48	8	25
41	46	32	50	42
45	24	1	21	34
14	35	49	12	4
7	44	20	29	47

Hearts Up, Clubs Down

Players: Two

Materials: Hearts Up, Clubs Down game sheet, scissors, tape, the suit of hearts and the suit of clubs from a deck of cards, a game marker for each player, pencil

Goal: Use the cards to add and subtract numbers.

Rules:

1. Cut apart the number lines on the game sheet. Tape the heart strip to the club strip. The number line should have the picture of the heart at the top and the club at the bottom. Each player puts his or her game marker on the zero.
2. Remove the face cards from the suit of hearts and the suit of clubs.
3. Shuffle the cards and deal them equally between the players.
4. Players keep their cards facedown in front of them.
5. Each player flips over one card from his or her stack. If the card is a heart, the player moves up the number line the same number of spaces as the number on the card. If the card is a club, the player moves down the number line.
6. Players continue flipping one card over at a time until there are no cards left. Then each player writes the number where he or she stopped on the score sheet. Be sure to include the plus (+) or minus (−) sign.
7. Players shuffle the cards again and continue playing.
8. At the end of the playing time, each player totals his or her score. Numbers with a plus sign are added and numbers with a minus sign are subtracted. The player with the highest score wins.

Math

Hearts Up, Clubs Down

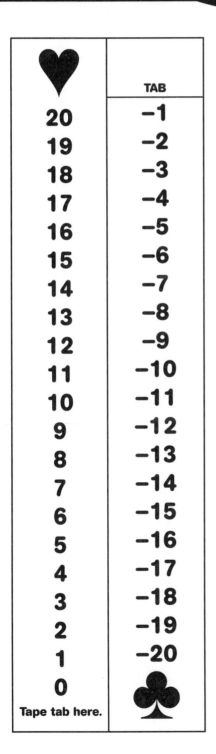

♥	TAB
20	**−1**
19	**−2**
18	**−3**
17	**−4**
16	**−5**
15	**−6**
14	**−7**
13	**−8**
12	**−9**
11	**−10**
10	**−11**
9	**−12**
8	**−13**
7	**−14**
6	**−15**
5	**−16**
4	**−17**
3	**−18**
2	**−19**
1	**−20**
0	♣

Tape tab here.

Score Card	
Team 1	Team 2

IF87060 *Brain Games*

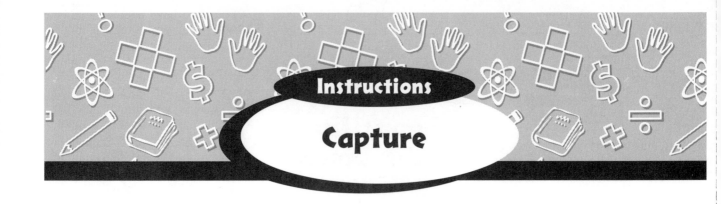

Capture

Players: Two

Materials: Capture game board, one deck of playing cards with the face cards removed, pencil and paper for each player

Goal: Use addition, subtraction, multiplication, and division to capture as many numbers on the game board as possible.

Rules:
1. Shuffle the cards and place them facedown in a pile.
2. The first player draws two cards.
3. The player uses the two numbers shown on the cards to create an addition problem, a subtraction problem, a multiplication problem, and if possible a division problem. The player writes the problems and answers on his or her paper.

   Example: The cards that are drawn show 10 and 2.
   $$10 + 2 = 12$$
   $$10 - 2 = 8$$
   $$10 \times 2 = 20$$
   $$10 \div 2 = 5$$

4. The player captures the answers to the problems on the game board. In the example above this would be the numbers 12, 8, 20, and 5. The player crosses the numbers out and writes his or her initials in the boxes.
5. Once a number has been captured, it cannot be captured again by any other player.
6. Players take turns capturing numbers until all of the cards have been used.
7. The player with the most captured numbers at the end of the game wins.

Math

Capture

1	2	3	4	5	6	7	8	9	10
11	12	13	14	15	16	17	18	19	20
21	22	23	24	25	26	27	28	29	30
31	32	33	34	35	36	37	38	39	40
41	42	43	44	45	46	47	48	49	50
51	52	53	54	55	56	57	58	59	60
61	62	63	64	65	66	67	68	69	70
71	72	73	74	75	76	77	78	79	80
81	82	83	84	85	86	87	88	89	90
91	92	93	94	95	96	97	98	99	100

IF87060 *Brain Games*

Digit Destination

Players: Two

Materials: Digit Destination game board for each player, pencil, one die

Goal: Roll the die and create three-digit numbers.

Rules:

1. The first player rolls the die and calls out the number.
2. Each player writes the number in either the hundreds place, the tens place, or the ones place on his or her game board. Players keep their game boards hidden from each other.
3. This is repeated until three numbers have been rolled. Then the players show the three-digit number they have written on their game boards. The player with the largest number wins the round and scores five points. If there is a tie, no one scores any points.
4. Play continues with the next player rolling the die.
5. The player with the most points at the end of the playing time wins the game.

Math

Digit Destination

	Hundreds	Tens	Ones	Score
1.				_____
2.				_____
3.				_____
4.				_____
5.				_____
6.				_____
7.				_____
8.				_____
9.				_____
10.				_____

Final Score _____

IF87060 *Brain Games*

Bigger Is Better

Players: Two

Materials: One deck of playing cards with the face cards removed

Goal: Use the playing cards to make three-digit numbers.

Rules:
1. Shuffle the cards. Place them facedown in a pile.
2. The first player draws three cards. He or she uses the numbers on the cards to create the largest three-digit number possible.
3. The second player draws three cards and uses them to create the largest three-digit number possible.
4. The player whose number is the largest wins all of the cards.
5. Play continues until there are no cards left in the pile. The player with the most cards wins the game.

Match Me

Players: Two

Materials: One geo board and several elastic bands for each player

Goal: Use the geo board to create shapes and patterns.

Rules:
1. The first player makes a pattern on the Geo board using three elastic bands.
2. The second player makes a matching pattern on his or her geo board.
3. If the patterns match, the second player creates a new pattern using four elastic bands.
4. The first player makes a matching pattern on his or her geo board.
5. At each turn, one more elastic band is added to the pattern. Play continues until one player is unable to create a match. The other player is then the winner.

Geo Mania

Players: Two

Materials: One geo board and several elastic bands for each player

Goal: Use the geo board to create shapes and patterns.

Rules:
1. Players sit with their backs facing each other.
2. The first player uses an elastic band to create a shape on his or her geo board. Then he or she tells the other player the name of the shape and where on the board it is located.
3. The second player must listen to the information and make the same shape in the same location on his or her board. Then he or she makes a new shape and tells the first player what it is and where it is located on the board.
4. Play continues until six shapes have been made on the geo boards. Then the players show each other their boards to see if they match.

Earn and Learn

Players: Two to Four

Materials: Earn and Learn game board, three copies of each page of Earn and Learn play money, file folder, glue, one die, one game marker for each player (beans, pasta noodles, pennies, etc.)

Goal: Earn money and pay bills on the way to the store.

Rules:
1. Cut apart the play money. Give each player 4 dimes, 2 nickels, and 2 quarters. Stack the rest of the money in piles and set them aside to create the bank.
2. Glue each side of the game board to the inside of a file folder.
3. All players put their game markers on "Start." The first player rolls the die and moves forward on the path that number of spaces.
4. The player reads the sentence and either earns more money or pays money out.
5. If the player does not have enough money to pay what he or she owes, the player loses a turn and must return to his or her last space.
6. Play continues until all of the players reach the store. The player with the most money wins.

Math

Earn and Learn

88

Earn and Learn

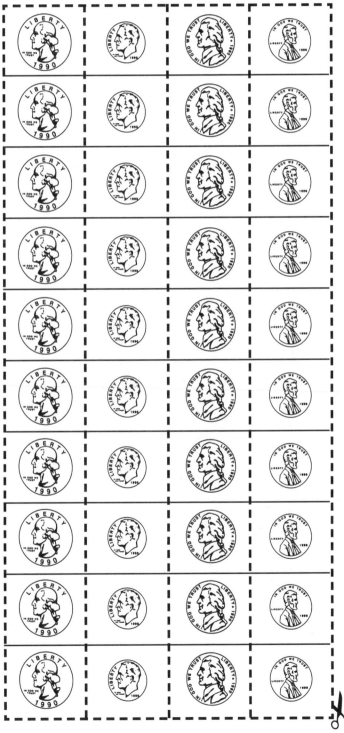

Math

Earn and Learn

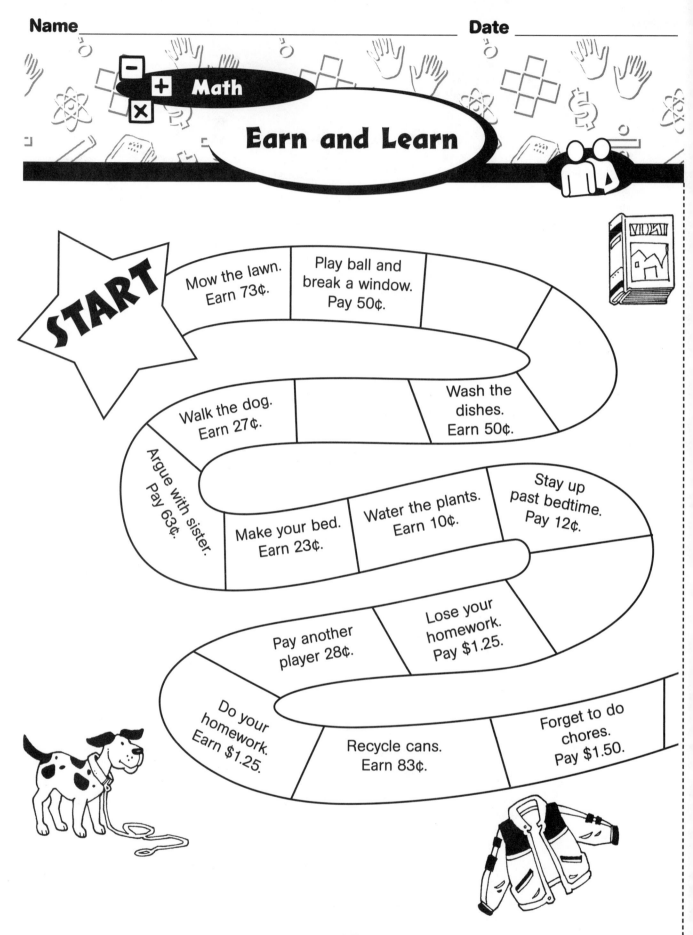

START

Mow the lawn.
Earn 73¢.

Play ball and
break a window.
Pay 50¢.

Wash the
dishes.
Earn 50¢.

Walk the dog.
Earn 27¢.

Argue with sister.
Pay 63¢.

Make your bed.
Earn 23¢.

Water the plants.
Earn 10¢.

Stay up
past bedtime.
Pay 12¢.

Pay another
player 28¢.

Lose your
homework.
Pay $1.25.

Do your
homework.
Earn $1.25.

Recycle cans.
Earn 83¢.

Forget to do
chores.
Pay $1.50.

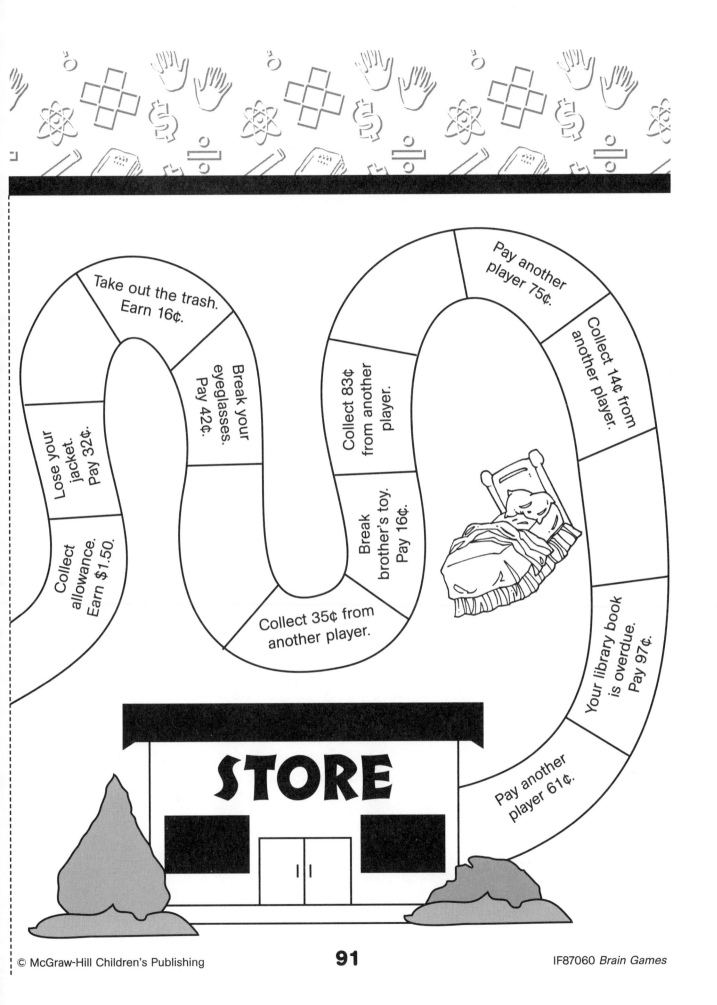

Take out the trash. Earn 16¢.

Break your eyeglasses. Pay 42¢.

Lose your jacket. Pay 32¢.

Collect allowance. Earn $1.50.

Collect 83¢ from another player.

Break brother's toy. Pay 16¢.

Collect 35¢ from another player.

Pay another player 75¢.

Collect 14¢ from another player.

Your library book is overdue. Pay 97¢.

Pay another player 61¢.

STORE

IF87060 *Brain Games*

Instructions

Trading Places

Players: Two

Materials: Trading Places game board, several copies of the Trading Places flashcards template, four game markers for each player (beans, pasta noodles, pennies, etc.)

Goal: Answer the questions on the flashcards to move across the game board and take over your opponent's home squares.

Rules:
1. Write a question and answer on one side of each flashcard. The questions can be about math, reading, science, social studies, or trivia. Cut the flashcards apart.
2. Shuffle the flashcards and place them facedown.
3. Each player claims one row of houses and places a game marker on each house in the row.
4. The first player draws a flashcard and reads the question to the second player. If the second player can answer the question correctly, he or she may move one game marker into an empty square. The markers can move forward, backward, left, right, and diagonally one square at a time.
5. The second player then draws a card and asks the first player the question on the card.
6. Players take turns asking and answering questions.
7. The first player to move all of his or her game markers into the opponent's houses wins the game.

Trading Places

Flashcards

IF87060 *Brain Games*

Critical Thinking

Trading Places

🏠		🏠		🏠	
🏠		🏠		🏠	🏠

IF87060 *Brain Games*

Brain Games

Entire-Class Games

IF87060 *Brain Games*

Players: Entire Class

Materials: Timer, pencil and paper for each player

Goal: Players write the most words beginning with a specific letter during a fixed period of time. Choose your time period based on grade level, range of class ability, and number of times this game has been played in class.

Rules:

1. Players are given three minutes to write as many words as they can that begin with the first letter of the alphabet (or a letter of your choice).
2. Encourage correct spelling but do not take off points for incorrectly spelled words.
3. The player who writes the most words wins three points.
4. Have players correct their spelling on their individual papers.
5. Players now write as many words as they can with a second letter of the alphabet. Continue as time permits.

Players: Entire Class

Materials: None

Goal: Players must complete a three-line sentence pattern, using words beginning with one specific letter of the alphabet. Sentence pattern is as follows:

> I am going to _____.
> On (in) a _____.
> To (do what)_____.

Rules:

1. Player #1 begins by using only words beginning with "A" in the pattern; for example, "I am going to Alaska in an airplane to act."
2. Player #2 uses only words beginning with "B" to fit the pattern; for example, "I am going to Boston on a boat to be a ballerina."
3. It may be helpful to write the three-line pattern on the board so students can follow it visually while creating their responses.
4. Split the class into two teams. Each team member who answers appropriately earns three points. Players who are unable to complete the three-line pattern miss a turn.
5. The team with the most points at the end of the game wins.

I Remember When

Players: Entire Class

Materials: None

Goal: Students will play with remembering something that used to be and now has changed. Students may need some coaching from you in initial responses or you could start by modeling an example of your own.

Rules:
1. All players begin with the sentence:
   I remember when _____, but now _____. It may be helpful to write this pattern on the board so that students may look at it while they are thinking of responses.
2. Divide the class into two teams.
3. Player #1 from Team One completes the sentence.
4. Player #1 from Team Two completes the sentence.
5. Play continues, with each team taking a turn until a player cannot think of a response.
6. If a player cannot think of a response, he or she misses a turn.
7. Each successfully completed sentence earns a point for the team.
8. The team with the most points at the end of the game wins.

Size Seekers

Players: Entire Class

Materials: None

Goal: Players will work with understanding comparisons by naming things that are smaller or larger than they are. All answers must refer to something living. You may act as the scorekeeper or, if you have uneven numbers for the team, you may assign a student scorekeeper.

Rules:

1. Organize the class into two teams.
2. Player #1 on Team One names something smaller than his/her own size; for example, a squirrel.
3. Player #1 on Team Two also names something smaller than Player #1.
4. Team members take turns until all members of both teams have had a turn. Then start again, with each team member having to name something larger than him/herself.
5. Each correct response earns one point.
6. If a team member is unable to come up with an appropriate response, the turn is lost.
7. The team with the most points at the end of the playing time wins.

 IF87060 *Brain Games*

Instructions
Winning Whispers

Players: Entire Class

Materials: None

Goal: Players practice their listening skills.

Rules:

1. Players sit in a circle. Explain the game to students, and make a special point of the fact that each player must listen carefully, since there will be no repeating of the whispered sentence. Each player gets one chance to listen.
2. Start the game by whispering a simple sentence into the ear of the player seated next to you on the left.
3. This player whispers what he or she has heard into the ear of the player on his or her left.
4. Play continues in this way until you call "stop." You may stop the game at any point.
5. The last player to hear the sentence repeats it out loud.
6. Announce the original sentence. Players will be able to see how well they listened.
7. Begin again with the next player in the circle.
8. Ask players to observe if listening improves with practice.

IF87060 *Brain Games*

Classification Classics

Players: Entire Class

Materials:

None

Goal:

Players will learn new phrases and will work at completing specific phrases given by the teacher.

Rules:

1. Read the beginning of each phrase and ask students to complete it.
2. Give students a specified time (such as one minute) to complete each phrase.
3. At the end of the game, ask students to share their responses to the class. In addition to sharing well-known phrases, you might want to also recognize creative responses, funny answers, etc.

Some phrases that can be used in this game include:

a team of_____	a gaggle of _____	a can of _____	a litter of _____
a field of _____	a pack of _____	a circle of _____	an ear of _____
a dozen _____	a group of _____	a bottle of _____	a mark of_____
a ball of _____	a piece of _____	a bundle of _____	a pledge of _____
a bunch of _____	a swarm of _____	a mug of _____	a change of_____
a life of _____	a drop of _____	a labor of_____	a breath of _____
a couple of _____	a herd of _____	a pile of _____	a member
a breed of _____	an ounce of_____	a work of_____	of _____
a pound of _____	a box of _____	a bowl of _____	a copy of_____
a cluster of _____	a gallon of _____	a ton of _____	a word of_____
a class of _____	a jar of _____	a collection	a handful of _____
a pinch of _____	a day of _____	of _____	

IF87060 *Brain Games*

Instructions

Cover to Cover

Players: Entire Class

Materials: One copy of the same edition of a newspaper for each team, pencil, and paper for each team

Goal: Teams investigate the newspapers and make observations.

Rules:
1. Divide class into teams of two.
2. Teams research a section of the newspaper chosen by you, making as many observations as they can about the information contained in the selected section.
3. Observations are recorded on paper by each team and shared with the entire class as a group. Each team has its own presentation time.
4. The team who makes the most correct observations at the end of the playing time wins. For example, in the movie section of the newspaper, players should be able to make the following observations: The time each movie is playing, the movie theater at which each movie is playing, the address of each movie theater, the phone number of each movie theater, the cost of tickets for adults and children, the rating of each movie, and a short description of each movie's plot.

Instructions
Twenty Questions

Players: Entire Class

Materials: One item you choose to place in the secret box

Goal: Players will identify an object in the "secret box" by asking questions.

Rules:
1. Divide class into two teams.
2. Teams take turns asking questions about the item in the secret box as they try to identify it.
3. No one may specifically ask the name of the object, but they can ask questions about the item that may help them to identify it. For example, questions such as the following may help with identification: What shape is it? Is it useful in the classroom? To whom is it useful? Do we all have one? To whom does it belong? Is it hard or soft? What is it made of? What color is it?
4. Questions are alternated between teams. Players can ask a total of twenty questions in trying to identify the item, with each team asking ten.
5. If a team member is successful in identifying the item, his or her team wins five points.
6. If no one is able to correctly identify the item after the twenty questions, then no points are earned. The secret item is shown to the class.
7. The game continues with a new item being placed in the secret box and new questions asked.
8. The team with the most points at the end of the playing time wins.

Players: Entire Class

Materials: Colored blocks (two of each color) for each player. Crayons can also be used.

Goal: Players work with positional words, such as *middle*, *left*, *right*, *between*, *under*, *above* and *below*, while learning to better follow directions.

Rules:
1. Players follow directions given by you, placing their colored blocks or crayons in different positions.
2. Be sure to give directions using the positional words listed above. Your directions could be similar to the following:

   Place a red block in the middle of your desk.
   Place a black block on the right side of the red block.
   Place a yellow block on the left side of the red block.
   Place a white block under the red block.
   Place a gray block on the left side of the yellow block.
   Place a dark green block between the yellow and the red block.
   Place a pink block above the yellow block.
   Place a blue block on the right side of the white block.
   Place a light green block above the red block.
   Place a purple block on the left side of the pink block.
   Place an orange block below the gray block.
   Place a brown block under the white block.

Eye Spy

Players: Entire Class

Materials: Paper and pencil for each player

Goal: Players strengthen their phonetic skills using this familiar old game.

Rules:
1. Choose a phonetic skill with which you feel students need practice; for example, the blend *sp*.
2. Use the phrase "I spy with my little eye something that begins with *sp*."
3. Players now search with their eyes for something that begins with sp. It could be a spelling book, a sponge, or a spider outside.
4. Players write down what they think your chosen item might be. Give a short time limit.
5. Players earn a point if they guess the item you had in mind correctly.
6. The player with the most points at the end of the game time wins.
7. Change your phonetic sound often as you play.

Players: Entire Class

Materials:

Paper and pencil for each player

Goal:

Players strengthen vocabulary and spelling skills by listing items related to specific categories.

Rules:

1. Choose one player to be the timekeeper.
2. Determine the playing time for each category.
3. Give players a category, such as animals.
4. Players list as many animals as they can within the time limit.
5. One point is earned for each correct response.
6. Give players a new category and follow the same steps.
7. Continue playing in this way as time allows.
8. The player with the most points at the end of the game time wins.

Some suggested categories you can use with this game:

animals	pets	toys	games
balls	snacks	fruit	vegetables
clothes	camping gear	flowers	trees
bugs	fish	birds	colors
boats	cars	desserts	states

A Tale of Truth

Players: Entire Class

Materials: Animal pictures

Goal: Players will expand their vocabulary and strengthen oral language skills by attempting to list as many characteristics of a given animal as they can.

Rules:
1. Divide class into two teams.
2. Place animal pictures in a pile, facedown.
3. Player #1 from Team One will choose the first picture, show it to the class, and proceed to tell something he knows to be true about the animal.
4. He will now pass the picture to Player #1 on Team Two, who will tell something he knows to be true about the same animal.
5. Players and teams take turns adding characteristics.
6. One point is earned for each correct response.
7. If a player is unable to answer or gives an incorrect answer, the picture is then passed on to the other team and no points are earned.
8. After a specified period of time, the game ends and the score will be totaled.
9. Begin again with a new picture.
10. The team with the most points is the winner.

Players: Entire Class

Materials: None

Goal: Players will learn about homonyms, words that are similar in sound but different in meaning. An easy way to remember what a homonym is the acronym HSS, which stands for "homonym, similar sound."

Rules:

1. Ask Player #1 on Team One to create a sentence using the first homonym on your list. If you are playing this game orally, be sure to spell each word.
2. Player #1 on Team Two must use the partner homonym correctly in a sentence.
3. Teams earn a point for each homonym used correctly in a sentence by one of its teammates.
4. If a player is unable to make a sentence or does so incorrectly, no points are earned and that player's turn is lost.
5. The team with the most points at the end of the playing time wins.

SUGGESTED HOMONYMS:

meat, meet	hair, hare	sum, some	eye, I
ring, wring	maid, made	right, write	our, hour
see, sea	won, one	knot, not	rap, wrap
through, threw	would, wood	new, knew	buy, by, bye
hear, here	so, sew	lie, lye	
week, weak	no, know	read, reed	
way, weigh	blew, blue	be, bee	
eight, ate	bear, bare	two, to, too	

Players: Entire Class

Materials: Pencils, paper, and crayons for students

Goal: Players will strengthen recognition of compound words by trying to make matches with words given by the teacher.

Rules:
1. Tell students to listen to a word you say. Ask them to try to make it into a compound word by adding another word to it. Students will write down each of their words.
2. Students may make the compound word by adding another word either before or after the teacher-prompted word.
3. Student papers can be recognized in a bulletin-board display after the game is over. If you like, you can ask students to decorate their finished game papers with drawings after the end of the game.

Here are some examples of words and compound matches that can be used in the game:

after (noon)	burn (sun)
ant (hill)	shell (sea)
arm (chair, rest)	walk (side, board)
back (bone, board, field)	ball (foot, base)
bath (tub, robe, mat)	book (cook, note)
bed (room, time, spread)	room (bed, home, bath)

Copycats

Players: Entire Class

Materials: None

Goal: Players test their memory by repeating a sequence of actions performed by previous players.

Rules:

1. Divide the class into groups of five.
2. Players stand in circles of five players each.
3. The first player in each group makes one action using either hands, feet, legs, or body.
4. Player #2 copies this action and adds one of his or her own.
5. Player #3 copies Player #2 and adds a third action.
6. The action continues around the circle until a player is unable to remember all of the moves in the sequence. That player sits down and leaves the game.
7. The game continues with the next person who can correctly repeat the sequence of actions.
8. The last person remaining is the winner.

Instructions

Animal Olympics

Players: Entire Class

Materials: None

Goal: Players strengthen categorizing skills and knowledge of natural science as they classify animals as *land dwellers*, *water swimmers*, or *sky flyers*.

Rules:
1. Divide the class into two teams
2. Select one of the animal categories for the first round of play.
3. Player #1 from Team One begins by naming an animal belonging in this category.
4. Player #1 from Team Two also names an animal belonging in this category.
5. Play continues with teams taking turns identifying animals belonging to the selected category. Team members earn one point for their team for each correct response.
6. If a player is unable to name an animal or makes an incorrect response, he or she loses a turn.
7. The team with the most points during a given period of time wins.
8. Start over by changing the animal category. If students seem stuck, you can change the category mid-round.

Players: Entire Class

Materials: None

Goal: Players will practice listening and following directions in drawing "Yankee Doodle Dandy" on the blackboard or whiteboard.

Rules:

1. Instruct players to listen carefully as you give directions. Explain that each direction will be given only once.
2. Choose a different player to complete each command.
3. Here is the list of instructions for players to draw:

a. Draw Yankee Doodle's head in the middle of the board.
b. Draw his body beneath his head.
c. Give Yankee Doodle a left leg.
d. Give him a right arm.
e. Put a nose on his face.
f. Give him a right ear.
g. Give him a left eye.
h. Put some hair on his head.
i. Give him a right leg.
j. Give him a mouth.
k. Draw some teeth in his mouth.
l. Give him a right eye.
m. Make Yankee Doodle's right hand.

n. Give him a striped pair of pants.
o. Draw his left arm.
p. Give him a right ear.
q. Draw his right foot.
r. Add eyelashes to his eyes.
s. Give Yankee Doodle a dandy ring.
t. Put a hat on his head.
u. Draw his left foot.
v. Design a spotted shirt for him.
w. Put a feather in his hat.
x. Make a collar for his shirt.
y. Design some boots for his feet.
z. Draw his left hand.

4. When the drawing is complete, ask everyone to sing the song "Yankee Doodle Dandy."

Instructions

Pantomime Time

Players: Entire Class

Materials: None

Goal: Students act out actions or situations connected to specific topics that are requested by you.

Rules:
1. Ask students to come to the front of the class one at a time.
2. Give each student a suggestion to act out. For example, a student may be asked to act out something that "can be done with the hands." This player can choose to do anything that might fall under that category, such as vacuuming, washing dishes, applauding at a concert, hugging etc.
3. Students must guess what is being pantomimed.
4. The first student who guesses the pantomime correctly becomes the player of the next pantomime.
5. Students will continue with a category until you change it.

Categories for this game can include:
things you do at home
things you do at school
things you do in the summer
things you do in the winter
games you can play
feelings or emotions

Follow Me

Players: Entire Class

Materials: None

Goal: Students learn to follow directions that include left and right commands. The directions can be simplified for younger players.

Rules:
1. Instruct players to listen carefully as you give directions. Explain that each direction will only be given one time.
2. Alert players to the fact that each instruction will include at least one left or right reference.
3. Here is a sample list of instructions for players to follow:
   a. Touch your right hand to your left ear.
   b. Touch your nose with your left hand.
   c. Put your right hand behind your back.
   d. Shake hands with the person on your left.
   e. Touch your right knee with your left hand and your left foot with your right hand.
   f. Lift your right foot off the floor and touch your right shoulder with your left hand.
   g. Put your right hand on your left knee, then turn in a circle.
   h. Put your left hand on your head and jump up and down on your right foot.
   i. Face left and put your right hand on the shoulder of the person in front of you.
4. Depending on your students' abilities, you might want to play along, complete the command after the majority of the students have completed theirs, or model a round before the game begins.

Players: Entire Class

Materials: Several objects small enough to place in a large paper bag. The more unusual the items, the better they will work for this game. You may want to bring in objects from home as well.

Goal: Students will gain practice in making observations by using the senses of touch, hearing, and smell to describe objects they cannot see. Players will see how important sight is in identifying many objects. They will also become aware of observations that are not possible without the aid of sight, such as color.

Rules:
1. Player #1 is blindfolded and removes an object from the bag.
2. Player #1 uses the sense of touch, hearing, and smell to make observations as he or she describes the object. Make sure the other students understand that they are not allowed to give hints, but only to observe and listen.
3. By making observations without the aid of sight, players will see if they can identify an item after a minimum of four observations. Here is an example: Player #1 removes a small wooden statue of a bird from the bag. Observations could include:
   "It has a hard surface."
   "It feels curvy and has one sharp end."
4. Once observations are concluded, Player #1 then tries to identify the item while still blindfolded.
5. Once the blindfold is removed, ask the player to make new observations by sight.
6. Continue play with the next student.

Walk About

Players: Entire Class

Materials: None

Goal: Players will practice listening and following directions while you guide them on an exploration of the classroom.

Rules:

1. Instruct players to listen carefully as you give directions. Explain that each direction will only be given one time.
2. Tell students that they will be looking for objects to touch, and that every object they need to find is in the classroom. Remind them that there will be multiple choices for each instruction, so they will not all head for the same object each time.
3. Here is a sample list of instructions for objects that players will find and touch:

a. Touch something soft.
b. Touch something high.
c. Touch something low.
d. Touch something with your left hand.
e. Touch something dark.
f. Touch something cold with your right hand.
g. Touch something round with your foot.
h. Touch something made of wood.
i. Touch something narrow with your elbow.
j. Touch something square.
k. Touch something comfortable.
l. Touch something red.
m. Touch something blue.
n. Touch something scientific.
o. Touch something written.
p. Touch something smaller than you.

Memory

Players: Entire Class

Materials: None

Goal: Players improve their sequential memory by building a sequence of actions with classmates.

Rules:

1. Player #1 touches an object in the classroom to start the game.
2. Player #2 touches the previous player's item and adds one.
3. Each player in turn must touch the items of previous players and keep them in the correct sequence.
4. If a player makes an error in sequencing, the game can continue if the next player can complete the original sequence correctly. If not, end the game and start a new one, with the next player starting a new sequence.

Imagine That

Players: Entire Class

Materials: Paper and pencil for each team

Goal: Players will strengthen their imagination and creative thinking skills by coming up with a list of uses for an ordinary object.

Rules:

1. Divide class into teams of two.
2. Tell the teams that you will show them an object. Tell them you want them to come up with as many uses for that object as they can think of.
3. Give students a specified period of time in which they will create their lists.
4. After they are done, have the teams share their lists. Teams will earn one point for each idea. The team with the most points wins that round of the game.

Example: Show the teams a piece of string. Responses might include:

Tie up a package with it.
Use it to make a piece of string art.
Use it to hold onto a kite when it is flying.
Use it for a tail in "Pin the Tail on the Donkey."
Use it to tie hair into a ponytail.
Use it as a belt for a pair of pants.

Instructions
False, True, or Neither Will Do

Players: Entire Class

Materials: Paper and pencil for each group

Goal: Students strengthen listening and critical thinking skills and will learn about the concepts of consensus and majority rule in decision-making.

Rules:

1. Organize the class into teams of four. Ask each team to choose one player to record the answers. The recorder will write the number of the question and then record the team response beside it. Tell the students that you will make a statement and they will make a decision on the statement by voting. This concept is called *majority rule*.
2. Players listen to a statement made by you.
3. Players use critical thinking skills to help them determine if the statement is *true*, *false*, or *neither*.
4. Players must decide as a team on one response to record.
5. The recorder will write *true, false,* or *neither* as the team's response for the question.
6. At the end of a set number of questions, ask teams to share their responses. Encourage students to explain their answers.
7. Now tell the class that you will play the game again. This time, however, the teams will use *consensus* to make decisions. This means that everyone on the team has to either agree with the answer or agree to allow an answer to be recorded even if they do not personally agree.
8. Deliver a set number of questions and extend the time period for decision-making.
9. After the round of play is over, encourage discussion about the two decision-making methods. Compare and contrast them.

Here are some sample statements to use in this game:
Lights turn things dark.
Boys are taller than men.
White things look cleaner than gray things.
A toddler is older than a kindergarten child.

Picture Perfect

Players: Entire Class

Materials: Paper and pencil for each player; assorted pictures or posters with a variety of detail in each one

Goal: Players will work at strengthening their observation for and memory of details seen in a limited period of time.

Rules:
1. Show players a picture or poster.
2. Allow students to view the picture for thirty seconds and then remove it from view.
3. Players list as many details as they can remember about the picture. After the players finish their lists, show the picture again. Players earn one point for each correct detail recorded. Allow time for guided discussion; did someone think the picture had a red car when in fact there was a red truck instead? Are there reasons that we think we see something that really is not there?
4. Begin the game again with another picture or poster. Have students notice whether their observation skills improve as the game continues.

Instructions

Shipwrecked

Players: Entire Class

Materials: Pencil and paper for each team list

Goal: Players refine reasoning skills as well as creative thinking and problem-solving skills in this game.

Rules:

1. Tell players they have been shipwrecked and are now on a desert island. Knowing that they have to survive several weeks without help, what one thing from the following list would they choose to have with them:

>an axe
>a box of matches
>a large container of water
>a battery-operated radio
>a fishing rod

2. Organize players into two teams based on their choices.
3. Each team lists as many reasons for their choice as possible. Reasons should include support for why they think their choice was the best one.
4. Groups then present their list of reasons to the class. Encourage classmates to ask questions after the presentation is finished.

Players: Entire Class

Materials: Guesstimate sheet for each player, one 12-inch ruler and a 30-inch or longer cloth measuring tape for each player

Goal: Players will learn the meaning of the term *estimate* and work with estimating and measuring skills.

Rules:

1. Give each player a copy of the Guesstimate sheet and a ruler and tape measure to begin the game. The ruler can be used to measure smaller objects, and the tape measure is for larger objects.
2. Briefly discuss the term *estimate* with the class. Explain that estimating is making an accurate guess about numbers, in this case related to the measurement of objects.
3. Players will work in pairs estimating the length of five to ten objects in the room. For the first round, you might want to assign objects; in additional rounds of the game, you may want to let students choose their own objects.
4. After each estimate, players will measure the object to check their accuracy.
5. Players record their estimates and measurements on the Guesstimate sheet.
6. Have players join together as a group to share their findings. Here are some sample discussion questions:
   - What can you tell us about your estimating?
   - What did you learn by measuring?
   - What were you most surprised to find?
   - What did you do differently as you continued to estimate and measure?

Math

Guesstimate

Object	Estimate in inches (or centimeters)	Measurement in inches
_____	_____	_____
_____	_____	_____
_____	_____	_____
_____	_____	_____
_____	_____	_____
_____	_____	_____
_____	_____	_____
_____	_____	_____
_____	_____	_____

Players: Entire Class

Materials: One set of 20 interlocking beads, cubes, or similar material for each player (Each set must be of the same type and size for each player. There should be several different colors within each set, but the colors need to be the same for each player. For example: A set could contain four blue, four red, four yellow, four green, and four black interlocking blocks. For convenience, store each set in a zippered plastic bag so it is readily available. These sets are useful in other activities related to math and patterning.)

Goal: Students practice patterning and memory skills with this hands-on activity.

Rules:
1. While students watch, model how you would connect three or four beads together.
2. When you are finished, hide your pattern from view and have students repeat the pattern from memory. Give a signal for the class to begin copying your pattern with their materials.
3. Set a time limit. At the end of the time, students will have the opportunity to compare their patterns with yours and make any necessary changes.
4. Begin the game again. Ask students to disassemble their patterns and watch while you create a new pattern for them to duplicate.

Instructions

Number Sequence

Players: Entire Class

Materials: None

Goal: Players will strengthen memory and patterning skills by using numbers.

Rules:
1. Divide class into two teams.
2. Ask Player #1 from Team One to repeat four numbers that you choose randomly. They can be any numbers in any order, for example: 23, 11, 42, 5 or 19, 7, 66, 20.
3. Player #1 must repeat the pattern of numbers correctly.
4. If Player #1 is correct, he or she earns a point for the team. If the player is incorrect, the play moves to Team Two.
5. Ask Player #1 on Team Two to repeat a pattern of four numbers.
6. After each turn, add another number to the sequence.
7. Play continues until your specified time period is up.
8. The team with the most points wins.

IF87060 *Brain Games*

Instructions

Worldwide Numbers

Players: Entire Class

Materials: Paper and pencil for each team

Goal: Players work cooperatively within teams to make a list of ways in which numbers are used in the world.

Rules:
1. Organize the class into four teams and hand out supplies.
2. Have students make a few sample suggestions that you write on the board. Guide the discussion by asking, for example, "How are numbers used in school?" Answers might include:
   > Numbers are used to tell how many students are present each day.
   > Numbers are used to tell what grade each class is.
   > Numbers are used for the school phone number to help people contact the school.
   > Numbers are used to teach students mathematics.
3. Allow teams to work independently. Set a time limit if you wish.
4. If students seem stuck, give a single suggestion to a team. For example, "How are numbers used at home?" Other suggestions could include: in sports, at the theater, in a car, in a newspaper, etc.
5. One point is scored for each appropriate answer on a team list.
6. Conclude the game with a group discussion. If you wish, you can complete the list on your blackboard or whiteboard together as an entire class.

Instructions

Before and After

Players: Entire Class

Materials:
None

Goal:
Players will work with before-and-after identification in number sequencing skills.

Rules:
1. Organize the class into two teams.
2. Name one team the "Before Team" and one team the "After Team."
3. Announce a segment of numbers with which the teams will be working for the first round of play. For example, 1 to 50, 50 to 100, 150 to 200, etc.
4. Ask Player #1 from the "Before Team" to choose a number within the range. For example, if you are working from 1 to 50, Player #1 might choose 30.
5. Player #1 from the "After Team" has to name any number that comes after 30 but falls within the designated range. For example, he or she could select 49, a number between 30 and 50.
6. Player #2 from the "Before Team" now has to name any number that falls before 49 in the designated range; for example, 25.
7. Play continues in this way until a selected time limit is up or a new category of numbers is selected.

Instructions

Believe It or Not

Players: Entire Class

Materials: Paper and pencil for each player

Goal: Players follow instructions and perform math processes.

Activity One:
Think of a number between 1
  and 10.
Write it down.
Double it.
Add 2.
Divide by 2.
Subtract the original number.
Surprise result:
  Everyone will have 1 as an
  answer.

Activity Two:
Think of a number between 1
  and 10.
Write it down.
Multiply it by 2.
Add 4.
Divide by 2.
Subtract the original number.
Surprise result:
  Everyone will have 2 as an
  answer.

Activity Three:
Think of a number between 1
  and 10.
Write it down.
Add 9.
Multiply by 2.
Subtract 4.
Divide by 2.
Subtract the original number.
Surprise result:
  Everyone will have 7 as an
  answer.

Activity Four:
Think of a number from
  between
  10 and 20.
Write it down.
Double it.
Add 5.
Add 12.
Subtract 3.
Divide by 2.
Subtract the original number.
Surprise result:
  Everyone will have 7 as an
  answer.

Activity Five:
Choose a number between
  10 and 20.
Write it down.
Double it.
Add 6.
Divide by 2.
Subtract the original number.
Surprise result:
  Everyone will have 3 as an
  answer.

Activity Six:
Choose a number between
  15 and 20.
Write it down.
Multiply by 2.
Add 8.
Divide by 2.
Subtract the original number.
Surprise result:
  Everyone will have 4 as an
  answer.

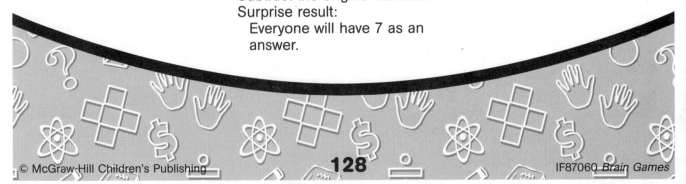

IF87060 *Brain Games*